Being Human

Hermie Medley

Hermie Medley

Being Human

Hermie Medley

Many Names Press
Santa Cruz, California

First Edition

ISBN 0-9773070-3-4 (ISBN-10)
ISBN 978-0-9773070-3-6 (ISBN-13)
Library of Congress Control Number: 2007923141

Cover Art © Samantha Green
Book Design © Many Names Press

Kate Hitt I Many Names Press
http://www.manynamespress.com/books
P.O. Box 1038 Capitola, CA 95010-1038 USA
Tel: 831-728-4302
khitt@manynamespress.com

Printed in the United States of America

Acknowledgments

Special thanks to Robin Medley and Megan Tresham for their help and support and to Dee Roe for her flawless opinions. In appreciation to Amber Coverdale Sumrall and her revision group for their constructive evaluations. Also gratitude to the writing groups and classes that have encouraged me over the years. My thanks to Samantha Green for the cover art and to Kate Hitt at Many Names Press who put it all together.

Dedicated to my son,
Steven Medley, 1949-2006

Table of Contents

Being Human

When I woke up this morning,
I noticed right away that I was still alive.
Grateful, I breathed in three enormous breaths,
stretched out my arms and listened
to that metronome, my heart. Outside,
I found the double redwood tree had also
made it through the night. Standing close
beside it, I couldn't see its head thrust
into the sky, just its lower limbs,
where a squirrel hustled along a branch,
level with my eyes. There we were—
the tree, the squirrel, and I, sharing
the game of life, they lilies of the field,
only I toiling and spinning, giving
thought to yesterday and tomorrow,
terrified of death and public speaking.

A December Day in May

I sit on the couch, swaddled in blankets.
It's spring, and the sun shines,
but I am dark as winter, my feet cold,
my blood sluggish. Every now and then
I have a day like this, a day of grieving,
over what I do not know.

Maybe it's for Molly, the kitten killed
by a neighbor's pick-up when I was five.
Maybe it's for my high school ring left
in a service station restroom, while I
was on a senior class field trip. Maybe
it's for my failure to complete my master's
degree, for just quitting one day and taking guitar
and writing classes at a junior college instead.

Maybe my grief is for my son, Peter, white
and lifeless at seventeen, after eight months
propped up by pillows in a hospital bed. Maybe
it's for my husband, killed when the plane
he was flying crashed into a strip farm
in Nebraska.

I don't know. Maybe I grieve for all
of these or perhaps for something else buried
deep in an inaccessible crevice of my psyche.

After a while I notice I'm not cold anymore. It's dark now. I get up from the couch and make myself a peanut butter sandwich on thick whole wheat bread. It tastes wonderful. I'm ready for a night of peaceful sleep, ready for the joy that comes in the morning.

Being Here Now

I was propped up in bed
in the middle of the afternoon,
reading a book by Ram Dass
about aging and dying. Suddenly
my attention was drawn to a show
going on outside my bedroom
window. The sprinkling system
was on, and water sprayed
the holly tree, the sun turning
each liquid droplet into a star
of light.

Exuberant as a bunch of naked boys
in a swimming hole, a flock
of small brown birds frolicked
in the tree, flying through the water,
bouncing on the pliant branches
with their glossy leaves, their clusters
of scarlet berries. I quit reading
about death and dying, got off the bed,
went for a walk in the afternoon sun.

Confession

I am not frightened so much
by the rumbling
of earthquakes, the roaring
of lions, the howling
of winter storms
as I am by the barely audible
whispering
of internal bogey men
telling me
in the night
what I do not want to know,
reminding me
of what
I do not want to remember.

Earthworm

I don't know how an earthworm
got into my house, but there it is,
expanding and contracting,
accordion-like,
on my indifferent rug.
Before long it just lies there,
motionless and resigned.

I think of other forms of life
uprooted from their natural habitats,
transplanted into foreign soil,
of the way they struggle to adapt,
only to give up and collapse,
devoid of hope, on whatever
carpet is their lot:

The oleander in the freeway's
center strip, subjected to dust
and gray exhaust fumes;
the lion, pacing in the circus cage
or jumping on command
through a trainer's hoops;
the young girl from Laos
in a California classroom
where no one speaks her language;
the old man in a rest home, bereft

of family and of choice,
picking listlessly at food he hates.

Tenderly I take the worm
out into the rainy night,
place it on a mound
of soft, black earth.

Hands

Can these hands, fragile as butterflies, be mine?
I sit on a park bench, stare at them, fingers entwined
on my lap. Can these blue veins, the crushed velvet skin,
marked with flecks of brown, belong to me? When I
was young, they played the piano, caressed a lover's
face, gave babies their morning baths. In my garden
I touched bark and water, soil and flowers
with these hands now weathered like ancient fences.
No longer are they the keys I once counted on
to open up my universe.

The sun is high and hot for early May. I feel the heat
seep through my blemished skin, warm my heart.
Holding a maple leaf, I trace the pattern of its veins.
An object slinks across the crewcut lawn. As it comes
close, I see it is a cat. It rubs against my foot, and though
 I hear no sound, I know that it is purring, because its tiny
motor resonates against my skin. I reach down, touch it
with my hands.

Spring in California

Some places spring comes in slowly,
the first sign, perhaps, a purple crocus,
pushing its chilly face up through the snow.
Here, spring arrives like wild fire, suddenly,
without notice. You look up
from your book, and there's not
just a solitary crocus but a landscape
broken out with flowers like a kid
with chickenpox. The sun runs an abnormal
temperature: birds sing in a different key.

I fall over oxalis in parking strips.
out to get anyone who questions their right
to take over the world. I steal rosebuds
from my neighbors' yards, because voices
tell me I must. I watch them open,
while my heart opens, too: stagger, giddy
from the greenness and wildness of it all.
I take a deep breath, unable to separate myself
from the sun, the sky,
the quickening pulse of the earth.

Generation Gap

Last night I had the strangest dream
I'd never dreamt before. I dreamed
I took my parents
to an open mike poetry reading
at the Santa Cruz Public Library.
I was eighty-three, which made my father
113, my mother 112. They were visiting,
and I thought they might enjoy
the poetry of the twenty-first century.

After half an hour of poems
with no punctuation and no form,
some of which sounded like a grocery list,
my father raised a palsied hand.
"You call this poetry?" he demanded.
"Where's the rhythm? Where's
the rhyme? Where's the story?"

He pulled himself up unsteadily
and worked his way to the podium,
his hair unkempt as a haystack.
"'Twas the 18th of April
in '75," he intoned. "Hardly a man
is now alive who remembers
that famous day and year."

He proceeded to recite the whole story
of how Paul Revere alerted his countrymen
that the British were coming. One
if by land and two if by sea
and all that malarkey. It had rhythm;
it had rhyme; it told a story. Everyone
was happy, I guess, though I'll never
know. Just as my father finished, I fell
out of bed and woke up in a heap on the floor.

What Do Parents Know?

"Don't change horses midstream,"
my parents used to tell me. "Why not?"
I wondered. A young girl,
working on the jig saw puzzle of life, I'd
stare out the window and watch the wind
bend the branches of the loquat tree
in our back yard. It seemed to me
the wind changed horses
whenever it felt like it. If it got tired
of blowing in one direction,
it blew in another.

The wind made things happen. The tree
which had been listing to the east
would begin to list to the west.
The flower pots on the patio
would topple to the left
instead of the right. The wind chimes
would switch from the key of F
to the key of A or C#minor. The fog bank
would lift and drift off to the sea.

Somehow I knew if the wind
were a person, it would never stay at a job
it hated: if it got sick of living in Seattle,
it would move to Denver, or wherever

it wanted to go. The wind would try
new hairdos, learn new languages,
climb higher mountains. It would not
just change horses. It would change
the direction in which the whole world
was moving.

Misreading Mother

Every time our family
loaded up its meager goods and moved,
with groundless optimism,
to a more unlikely spot, we left behind
a garden. Beets and carrots, yes,
but more important to my mother,
delphiniums, pansies and sweet peas
clinging to a wire trellis.

When in 1930 we finally bought
a southern Oregon farm, she planted
pink geraniums, the dishes still unpacked.
She had no gift for cooking, seldom dusted,
never learned to knit. Though neighbor
women would get together for an afternoon
of rummy, my mother looked on cards
as tools of the devil. But she filled our yard
with flowers. Bees hovered over mock orange,
pinks and columbine. Butterflies
poised on purple lilac clusters. In spring
the smell of honeysuckle, climbing
up the clothesline poles, made me dizzy.

I can see my mother in her shapeless house dress
on her knees beside the kitchen door,
digging in the soft black earth, hear her singing

Rock of Ages a bit off-key,
as she divided the iris. She liked
old fashioned flowers—cosmos, asters,
daisies, and chose them, I supposed, because
they were simple and straight forward,
just as I perceived her.

But looking back I wonder,
for above all else, she valued her oriental
poppies, red and black and sensual,
flowers for a gypsy or a femme fatale,
for someone filled with mystery
and longing.

I Didn't Touch Them

When I went home from college
at Christmas vacation, there
they were, waiting for me
at the train depot,
my mom and dad, their faces
like lighted candles. I climbed down,
clutching my winter coat
as though it might get away,
positive they could tell
I was not their little girl anymore,
knew I'd quit believing
in God, knew that I drank beer.
I wanted to say, "Don't hate me.
I can't stand it if you hate me,"
but I just stood there, hard
as a piece of fire wood.
I didn't touch them,
just watched
as their candles went out.

Memory, 1932

Southern Oregon, a warm May afternoon.
Bees buzz in azalea blossoms; robins build nests
in towering pine trees. Students stare out
the windows of the two-room country school,
some with faces innocent as babies, some
with pimples of adolescence. School will be out
in three more days. For the last fifteen minutes
students have been waiting for the closing bell
to ring. No one studies. They whisper, laugh,
scrape their feet on the rough wooden floor.
Someone throws a paper airplane
right past the teacher.

She doesn't notice. Young, her pink rayon dress
short and tight, her lips bright crimson, she is filing
her fingernails. She will not be coming back next
year. The students don't know why. Some have
heard it has to do with Clarence Able's father.
The bell rings. The students dash through the door, out
into the yard, full of sun, bees and robins.

After All These Years

Last night I dreamed of a November in southern
Oregon. A high school freshman, I stand beside
the mailbox, waiting for the school bus. The sleeves
of my shabby winter coat end a couple of inches
above my wrists. Frost covers the alfalfa pasture,
the black roof of our house. Red and yellow maple leaves
cascade over my head and carpet the road.
It's so cold I can hardly grip the binder holding my
carefully completed homework.

This November morning I awaken in California.
No frost, no bright maples here, but out at the end
of the driveway a liquid amber blazes with red
foliage. Dozens of leaves land on my old Ford. I
drive off, carrying autumn with me. The leaves fly
into the air, fall randomly onto indifferent streets.
And I remember my dream, how I once stood
under maple trees, my mind, then as now,
full of poems waiting to be born.

The Stone

At five o'clock he came home with the kids,
their faces pink from wind and sunshine,
trailing sand across the kitchen floor.
He hugged me by the stove,
where I was stirring onions in a skillet.
Into my palm he pressed a round, hard object,
closed my fingers around it one by one.
"For you," he said, then left to bathe the kids.

Opening my fingers, I found a small gray stone,
worn to smoothness in the tumbler of the sea.
It fit my hand the way a kitten
fits the body of its mother.
I saved it in my jewelry box to share its life
with assorted rings and brooches.

After the kids were grown and he was gone,
it rested there among the pearls and diamonds
until one day I took it from the box,
my fingers dry as fallen leaves,
placed it on a windowsill
beside a pine cone and two owl feathers.

To my Son, Peter

When Mary's son hung on the cross,
the land was covered with darkness.
When he died, the curtain of the temple
was torn in half, the earth convulsed
by earthquakes.

During your last hours,
the land was covered
with sunlight.
When you died, bees buzzed
over wild lilacs, larks warbled
in the trees.

I'd have preferred for the sky to weep,
the wind to shriek and howl,
at least for spring to hang its flag
at half mast for the day.

Hardwired

I woke up this morning wanting
to knit a scarf, a russet scarf
with fringe. This was no casual wanting
but a smoking flame of need, the kind
I used to have when I was pregnant.

Then I'd knit blue baby blankets
for days while a tiny embryo floated
in my briney inner sea, throwing off
my hormones and filling me
with strange, quixotic longings.

Well, I can't blame it anymore on babies,
the way I get demented
every now and then, write poetry all night,
take up the ukulele, plant fourteen pots
of amaryllis bulbs, dance the tango
by myself around the living room. When
this morning's urge to knit grabbed me
by the throat, I went out in a downpour,
purchased yarn and needles for a scarf,
a russet scarf with fringe.

Hemingway, Notwithstanding

"Love is also a good subject," Hemingway
wrote to Scott Fitzgerald. Maybe so,
but a better subject might be tomatoes.
No one beats his wife because tomatoes
drive him to it. Tomatoes do not cause
a pom-pom girl to offer up her body
to the captain of the football team.

Tomatoes do not take you captive, nor
is a tomato field a hotbed of land mines.
They do not hold a dagger to your breast,
nor burn big, jagged holes in the paper
as you write. Take love as a subject,
if to do so makes you happy. As for me,
I'll write about tomatoes.

A Letter to my Acupuncturist

Dear Donna, when you told me Las Vegas
would deplete my *chi* you
were right. That place was as plastic
as a fast food container, our hotel
a phony pyramid, full of cigarette smoke
and an air conditioned nastiness
that challenged my sinuses. Getting anywhere
required walking through acres
of gambling machines, watching
gray-faced robots trying compulsively
to beat an unbeatable system. Flashing lights
and relentless noise turned everything
surreal. And there I was, stuck
in the middle of an ugly, treeless desert.

But that was four days ago, and now
I'm in Yosemite Valley. I drove
along the Merced River this morning, pleased
to find it real, not some rinky-dink,
man-made waterway, posing
as a Venetian canal. I gulped big breaths
of clean, unconditioned air. I looked up
at the cliffs, and they are made of granite,
Donna, not papier mâché. The trees
are genuine wood. Bridal Veil Falls isn't run
by an electric motor. I feel the *chi*
moving through my body once again, Donna.
A few of your needles, and I'll be myself again.
Love, Hermie

Later Than Mid-life Crisis

One morning in April about the time
I started getting real, two friends and I
put on our best church suits, our mid-heel
pumps, and went for a day in the City.

On Geary Street we chanced into
a gallery where a small group of Chagalls
hung on exhibit. Viewing the paintings
of flowers, circus scenes, donkeys
suspended in the air, suddenly I ached
to climb out of my box, live a life
of color, metaphor, and dream. And,
oh to throw off gravity, hover upside down
beside the moon, while the man on the roof
played his violin.

"Oh, my God!" I cried. "Look at the barn
on fire! Look at the chickens!" My friends
moved to the next room, pretended
not to know me. I didn't care. "Look," I
ordered the world at large. "Just look
at the bride and groom floating free."

Identity Crisis

This morning when I turned on
my computer, it stuck out its tongue
at my password. At Safeway
the ATM machine refused to honor
my numbers, forcing me
to write a check.

In the check-out line I stood behind
a woman I was sure I knew. No spark
of recognition lit up
her concrete face. Even when I identified
myself, it was clear she couldn't
recall me, though she'd shared
the grim details of her hysterectomy
at Dolores Chávez's birthday bash
less than a week before.

My heart pounded with apprehension. Maybe
someone had stolen my identity. Maybe
I wasn't myself anymore. I rushed
for my car and headed for home
so upset I ran over a curb
getting out of the parking lot. Once
in the house, I stood in front
of my full length mirror. What
a relief! I was still myself—

with the same white hair, the same
dirty glasses, the same
thick middle. Only one thing
was different—the big, blue knot
on my forehead, a consequence, I decided,
of running head-on into life.

Don't Think Twice

It's the late 1960s.
Bob Dylan's on the radio.
Don't think twice he tells me,
but I can't help myself.
I think not once, not twice,
but at least a thousand times,
as I twist and turn each night,
sheets pulled up from the bottom
of the bed, mind as out of control
as crab grass.

Will my younger son flunk English,
my teen-age girl get pregnant?
Will the war be over soon,
or will my older son be drafted,
his remains sent home from Viet Nam
in a body bag? Is he smoking pot
at college? Does my husband have a lover
on the side? Will the money stretch enough
to pay both taxes and tuition?

Who is Dylan to tell me
how often I should think?
Does he have three kids,
a mortgage, plus a mole on the left side
of his neck that looks like it might

be growing? Does he wake up every morning
drenched in menopausal sweat?
By God, I'll think as often as I want,
and, no matter what you say, Bob,
it's not all right.

Backyard Infidel

What I'm writing is blasphemy,
and it would come as no surprise,
if, as my pen moved across the page,
God were to strike me dead.
I'm attacking a tradition
as hallowed as Easter morn –
the holy, blessed, sacrosanct
American barbecue.
It's November, and Webbers
all over the land have been stored
inside garages.
Barbecue season is over,
And I'm glad, glad, glad.

Since early April any social events
worth their salt and pepper
have involved gargantuan slabs of meat,
cooked on the spot by the Lord
of the Grill—John Wayne, playing with fire.
Inside he can't toast a piece of bread,
but on the deck, in his chef's hat,
he evolves into an expert.
He knows his cuts: he knows his fuels.
He could write a book on sauces.
With verve he wields his fork:
and when the job is done, serves up

the meat—from bloody sirloin
to blackened T-bone steak.

During barbecue season
I eat before I go. But now it is November,
and the Webbers are hibernating.
The time for Christmas fruit cake looms
just around the corner.

The Eighth Day

After God had made the universe,
Created man in his own image,
He observed his handiwork
For several generations.
And boy, was he disgusted!
First Adam and Eve defied him,
Then Cain killed Abel in a fit of rancor.
Since then things had only gone downhill.
Humans were getting nowhere,
Just slouching in the desert,
Clobbering one another, herding sheep.
So God put his foot down.
"Enough of this,"he bellowed.
"Life is more than bread.
Create yourselves some roses.
Sing, dance, make some hieroglyphics."
Thus creativity was born,
And what a mixed bag that turned out to be—
Paleolithic symbols scratched on cave walls,
Michelangelo's frescoes in the Sistine Chapel,
Salome's dance to gain the head of John the Baptist,
The Bolshoi ballet, the Charleston,
The sound of drums rising from the jungle,
Children's voice singing in a choir,
Tales around the fire,
The *Iliad* and *Howl*.
And God, seeing it was good,
Blessed the eighth day.

Recovery

George's eyes light up
when he talks about his men,
prisoners he teaches
at the County jail.
Most are alcoholics,
and they're learning
to write poetry, he says.

When I met George,
he'd been sober for less
than a year and couldn't yet
look people in the eye,
but, at least, he'd quit living
in the ruin of his van
and had almost forgiven
his drunken mother for dying
at the age of twenty nine.

Today George hasn't had a drink
for over twenty years.
He smiles when he talks
about his men. "They need poetry
in their lives," he says,
looking straight into my eyes.

Dressing for the Season

Though I am an old woman, I do not
wear purple. Purple
speaks of spring, of crocuses
breaking through the snow. Purple
makes unfounded promises, dreams
unlikely dreams.

Now late in the autumn of my life
I dress myself from head to toe
in brown. Brown with its Mona Lisa
smile has much to remember.
It is the color of completion,
the tying up of sheaves. Black
may be the signature of death,
but rich shades of brown—
umber, russet, bronze—
are the colors of fulfillment.

Ellie

The first few months Ellie was in my class, she spent
most of her time pretending she was smoking. So
strong was her addiction that she lit cigarettes, one
after another, inhaled deeply, filled the classroom
with clouds of pretend smoke. Then one day
she quit cold turkey and never smoked again.

Ellie suffered from Down's Syndrome as well as
a chronic heart disorder that gave her a red and
mottled face, blue lips and fingernails. I taught her
living skills, how to comb her sparse, limp hair,
how to tie her shoes and set the table, but I didn't
have to teach her how to live. She'd figured that
out by herself.

To school dances, Ellie, in her early teens, would
come dressed in her finery, mouth painted scarlet,
hair shaped in ringlets with a curling iron. And
she'd dance every dance, the belle of Gateway
Center's ball.

To this day I can see her beating on a tambourine
to *Jesus Met the Woman at the Well.* Sometimes
her enthusiasm called for a little curbing. At the zoo
she tried to get into the llama's cage. Once we lost
her on a field trip. When we found her, she was
sitting at the bar of the Green Hut, ordering
a margarita.

Faces of Time

Time flows like a river bent for the sea,
hangs in the sky like the waning moon,
sifts through life's fingers, kernels of sands,
casts no shadow upon the ground.

Time fights the bit like an unbroken horse,
drags its feet like a truculent child.
It leaves its tracks in the new fallen snow,
whispers dark threats on tropical nights.

Time's a magician with a bag full of tricks:
Time's a liar who remakes the past.
It weaves a dream, a gossamer trap.
Perhaps time is God winking his eye.

Change in the Weather

Like him, the day, at first, kept its promises.
The sun leapt over the horizon: a breeze
stirred the fringe-like strands of the willows,
a few dollops of white cloud meandering
overhead. Later, like him, the day changed
its mind. Clouds blackened, eclipsed the sun:
rain pounded the earth: the breeze turned
vicious. Ropes of willow branches slammed
across the landscape, left remnants
of a sacred covenant.

I Do Not Like Green Eggs and War
(With apologies to Dr. Seuss)

I'm twenty two.
My name is Joe.
In case of war I would not go.

When would you heed your country's call?
—Not in summer, not in fall.
I would not heed the call at all.

Would you go in ice and snow?
—The answer to that question's *no*.
I would not go in ice and snow.
I would not go at 10 below.
I'm telling you my name is Joe.
There's no weather would make me go.

Would you go near or far?
Would you go in a trolley car?
—How absurd your questions are!
I would not go near or far.
I would not go in a trolley car,
not aboard a shooting star,
not through the mail in a mason jar.
As I said, "My name is Joe.
There is no way that I would go.

Would you go to war in Spain?

In rain that's falling
in the plain?
—No, I would not go to war in Spain.
I would not fight in Bangor, Maine.
Not in China nor Iraq,
I would not fight in Hackensack.
I would not fight in Ireland
nor in the hot Sahara sand,
not in Idaho nor Delaware.
I would not fight war anywhere.

I'm twenty two.
My name is Joe.
In case of war I would not go.

Still Blocks Away

It's my 84th birthday. Several family members
meet me at the Bagelry for a midmorning snack.
My granddaughter talks the waiter
into putting four candles on my three-seed
bagel. I blow them out with only two tries.

There's a big sloppy warm place
inside me. Outside the sun is shining
in the January sky. Camellias are in bloom—
pink, white, and that deep, dark red
they claim is theirs alone. Later
I plan to take a walk
beside the ocean, watch
it play leap frog along the cliffs.

After my family leaves, I read
the morning paper. Thirty-five American soldiers
have been wounded
by an Iraqi mortar attack. Mad cow disease
has reached the United States. California faces
huge budget cuts. Over half the population
is overweight. Children are starving
everywhere.

Though I feel close to tears for all the misery
in the world, I realize with a certain amount
of guilt that the big ball of happiness

still sits in my stomach, refusing
to go away. I drive toward the ocean.
Still blocks away, I can hear
waves crashing with joy
against the rocks.

Admission

I am a serial killer of Boston ferns,
Though not by design.
I see them, green and graceful,
In the homes of others,
Obsessively desire them,
Though any Boston fern
Dependent on my care,
Will die a slow and lingering death.
In the shade or in the sun,
Overwatered, unwatered,
Tended or ignored,
It will die.

I tell myself I've watched enough
Of them turn brown,
Their leaves fall, dry
And lifeless, to the floor,
Leaving naked skeletons.
I promise myself not to take another victim.

Then one day I find somehow
Another fern has made its way
Into my shopping cart,
Headed for the lethal chamber of my home,
Doomed to end up as a corpse
In my backyard cemetery.
I want to take it back,
But I can't.

Margarita's Prayer

Dios, nos bendiga
help us cross this highway.
We cower at the roadside
with our two little sons.
The yellow lights of cars and trucks
shine in the dark for miles.
They look like golden Christmas ornaments
strung along the border.
We stand so close,
waiting for an opening,
we can feel the cars' vibrations
in our bones.
Our hearts are pounding hard.
We cling to one another
and the plastic bags that hold
everything we own.

The money his brother sent us
is strapped to Pablo's waist.
We'll pick *manzanas* in Washington.
Our boys will have new *zapatos*.
They will never cry again
from hunger in the night.
But first we have to get across
this highway. *Dios, por favor*
stop the traffic, like you parted
the sea for Moses. Help us
enter safely
a new and better land.

I Was Born in January or Maybe It Was July

The day had been so bad that I went to bed at seven o'clock out of pure frustration. I lay there, thinking of how my once faithful memory now betrays me. Imagine not being able to bring up the name of either the New York college my youngest grandson has been attending nor the European country, that begins with an "I", where he'll be a student this coming year. Much as I hate to admit it, I can't even remember his name half the time. Today I wasted forty dollars on taxi fare as well as most of the morning going to the dentist on Wednesday, when my appointment was really on Friday. It's no fun being recall-challenged, I can tell you.

The next morning I phoned the doctor's office. When I told the secretary it was an emergency, she let me come in an hour later. "I want my memory back," I told the doctor. "How long should that take?"

"I'm sorry." he said, "but there really isn't a whole lot I can do. I'm a doctor, not a magician. You're really in pretty good shape for someone 86 years old."

I wasn't pleased. I didn't like the way he herded me toward the exit like I was a cow.

"I've had enough of this," I told my daughter that afternoon. "I want to know what day it is. I want to know it seven days a week. I want to remember my birth date, address, telephone number, the names of all my grand children. I want you to help me find a more competent doctor, one who'll bring my memory back—and accepts Medicare."

"I'm afraid there ain't no such critter," she said, kissing me on the forehead. She picked up the daily paper and looked at the front page. "Is today really Thursday?" she asked, her forehead all scrunched up. "I could have sworn it was Friday."

Acceptance

By October, the year, matronly and gray at the temples, is suffering from mid-life crisis. Her orchards are heavy with apples, her fields orange with pumpkins and golden with ripened wheat. Air from smoky bonfires fills her lungs as she walks through showers of bright falling leaves. Mornings are chilly, mid-days warm, evenings aglow with the star-filled sky. One night, unable to fall asleep, she is overcome by sadness, nostalgic for spring when she was young and giddy, for summer with its languid afternoons. Time is running out: winter lies ahead—drab, cold, and final. The harvest moon floats above the hills: crickets chirp in pastures. She realizes, even without her, the seasons will carry on as they always have. She has played her part, as best as she was able. Her body relaxes: she falls asleep, peaceful as though swaddled like a baby.

The Driftwood Bird

When I found it on the beach, I stuck it in the buggy with the baby, later pushed them both home in the thin February sun. The cocker spaniel ran along beside us, making an occasional wild dash toward the sea gulls scavenging in the sand. When the baby learned to walk, we had to get rid of the dog, because it bit him on the face. Later we had to let the baby go, too, because first he entered college, then grew up and left home for good. I still have the driftwood bird, have moved it from home to home for over fifty years. It sits on a shelf, its wooden Pinocchio beak sticking out into the living room. I suspect most of my visitors wonder why I keep this ancient souvenir, treat it as a guest of honor. To me it is a symbol, as the dried camellia corsage from her junior prom is to a romantic girl. When I look at the bird, it's 1950 again, and we are living on the Oregon coast, high above the Pacific Ocean. I kiss my husband goodbye in the morning as he leaves to teach at the high school in Tillamook. Later I shape the towel into big rabbit ears, as I dry the baby's head after his bath. I sing to him from *The Fireside Book of Folk Songs* before his nap. His face lets me know his favorite song is the one about Dublin's fair city, so we have that one every day. In the afternoon, if the weather's in a good mood, we go down to the beach where we'd found the bird. Later, when my husband comes home, he lifts the baby to his shoulders

and gallops him around the house, or, if the baby is
teething and fussy, sings *Beer, Beer for Old Willamette U*
to help him fall asleep. As I watch them, I'm convinced
life is beautiful, about as beautiful as it gets. Today,
so many years later, looking at the driftwood bird, I
know that I was right.

Please Pass the Potatoes

For a couple who came from a Kansas house with a sod roof, my parents had standards for table manners higher than a silo. When my four brothers and I were growing up, we lived on a small Southern Oregon farm at the time the Depression was vigorously throwing its weight around. While many of our neighbors went on welfare, because of our few acres of black soil, we always had enough to eat without resorting to public assistance. Our meals consisted of fruit and vegetables raised in our own garden, eggs from our chickens, and milk from our cow, Josephine, plus lots of rice and dry beans purchased at Piggley Wiggley Market in nearby Grants Pass. In our ancient wood stove, my mother baked about a dozen loaves of bread each week, which tended to dry out before the next batch was due. Though her cooking was plain, devoid of spices and imagination, none of us ever went to bed hungry. And that's where good table manners come into this story.

My parents believed them to be a way of expressing gratitude that God was watching out for us. So my mother saw to it that we set the table properly—forks and napkins on the left of the plates, knives and teaspoons on the right. We children were expected to come to meals with clean hands and faces, to sit without slouching. Before we ate, my father would ask one of us to say grace. My favorite started "God is great; God is good, and we thank him for this food," and it was the one I always said. Next we'd pass the bowls of food around until all were served. As we ate, we were expected to take part in appropriate conversation without talking with our mouths full.

My father had a Bible verse he'd use, if our talk did not meet his standards. "If there be any virtue and if there be any praise, think on those things." He had two other rules at meals, as well: "Never sing at the table, and be sure to thank your mother for cooking the meal." No one left the table until all were finished.

Sometimes I found the whole process boring. Why did my father have to make such a federal case out of mealtimes anyway? Why did we always have to sit there while slowpoke Dean chewed each bite about 500 times? It wasn't until much later that I realized how much I was affected by the way our family made a rite of those simple meals. To this day I like to eat in a peaceful environment, hate loud restaurants, can't stand it if forced to listen to a football game during dinner. Sometimes I find myself saying internally that old grace I chose when I was eight, now thanking the Creator not just for food but for the gift of life itself.

Breaking God's Heart

When I was not yet two, my straight-laced Methodist parents played some not-very-straight-laced music on a tinny, 1920 phonograph. They'd lift me up onto their big double bed where I'd dance in perfect rhythm, swinging my diapered rear-end with abandon. This practice didn't last long, as they feared I might continue dancing beyond the age of innocence.

I hadn't danced for years when I started to high school, but my parents took me aside for a serious discussion of the matter. My father explained that though God hadn't minded when I danced alone as an innocent baby, His heart would be broken were I to start dancing now with members of the opposite sex. When he uttered the word "sex," my mother turned brilliant red from neck to hairline. I assured them I wouldn't dance with any boys, as I found boys disgusting, and besides, I didn't want to break God's heart.

After high school I entered a Methodist college, giving my parents a false sense of security. The first weekend I went to a mixer, which turned out to be another word for dance. Boys seemed to have changed, not routinely disgusting like the ones I'd previously known. When I confessed I'd never learned to dance, they told me to just fake it, which I did. I loved the beat of the music as it throbbed in my body, the feel of my partner's hand pressed against my back. I floated around the room, my heart pounding in my chest.

The next week I went to a dance at my dorm. "Could this be wrong?" I asked myself, as I moved in exquisite unity with a redheaded freshman. As we danced by a picture of Jesus on the wall, he seemed to look right at me with an approving smile.

"Of course it's not wrong. It's just fine," I would have sworn he told me, his hands raised in a blessing.

In the Beginning and Ever Since

After God had finished the heavens and earth, he put his hands on his hips and viewed his handiwork. "Not too shabby," he told himself. "I like these trees and plants; these birds and beasts are fine, but it seems to me something is missing." He pulled on his long white beard, and, flash, it came to him. He ought to make some people, but that, of course, was risky. He'd better go about producing them with caution. Just one would be enough to start with. So God formed man out of the dust and breathed into his nostrils the breath of life. And he named the first man Adam and stuck him in the garden on his own to sink or swim.

Adam was prepared for life like a baby is for college. He couldn't cook except to barbecue; he put too much detergent in the washing machine, didn't call his mother on her birthday, and forgot to send his gray suit to the cleaners. His doctor said his heart showed signs of stress. God had mercy on poor hapless Adam, and while he was asleep, removed one of his ribs and turned it into a laundress and a cook, a gopher and a social secretary. God called this handy thing a woman and gave her unto Adam. With Eve around, his life went much more smoothly, and his heart got better right away. He found she could also warm his feet at night, and with a job, help pay the mortgage, and that was fine with Adam, as long as she served dinner on the dot of six o'clock and didn't have the gall to earn a paycheck larger than his own.

Paul Had it Right on the Button

The night after I signed up for a writing group on spirituality, I was unable to fall asleep. Whatever had given me the notion I knew anything about the subject anyway? I couldn't even tell you what spirituality is, let alone write a poem about it. I crawled out of bed and pulled the dictionary off the shelf. Head propped on two pillows, I looked up "spirituality" in my decrepit old Webster's.

"The state of being spiritual", it informed me.

"Oh, thanks a lot," I replied. Then I looked under some related words until I found where it said that spirit is the part of the human being associated with mind and feeling, as distinguished from the physical body. That sounded pretty good to me. It made me think of my father, who always watched his thoughts and behavior. When any member of his family got negative, he'd quote from one of his favorite parts of the Bible,

"Whatsoever things are honorable, whatsoever is just, whatsoever is pure, whatsoever is lovely, whatsoever is gracious, if there is anything worthy of praise, think about those things."

Even though St. Paul was a male chauvinist pig in my uncharitable opinion, I realized his spiritual advice is what I've tried to practice most of my life. I dropped the dictionary on the floor and fell asleep in less than five minutes.

Keeping the Dog In the Yard

All my life fear and worry have been like an outside dog, ever alert to get inside, if the door's left open even an inch or two. When I was a little girl, one fear was of the ocean, of waves plotting to sweep me off to sea. I'd wait until the tide went out, then creep across the wet sand to see what the ocean had left behind—driftwood, a wooden box, a dead bird, a worn-out canvas shoe.

Later my fear was of alleys, where I worried some bad man, stalking young girls on their way to school, might jump from behind a tree. My heart would thud in my bony chest as I planned, should the need arise, to clobber him over the head with my red, aluminum lunch box. When I reached adolescence, I lay awake at night worrying whether I'd be picked to edit *Tokay*, the high school annual, be accepted by Willamette, the only college to which I'd applied.

A few years later, it was a great relief when World War II ended, making it possible for me to marry a certain lieutenant and have the first of my children before I was thirty. There were days when motherhood and worry seemed almost synonymous. Was the little one running a fever? Had the middle one forgotten to take her lunch money to school? Was the oldest one fooling around with pot?

And it kept right on, as the years went by, only with different questions. Had I turned off the oven before I left home? Would the reign of this President last forever? Would my great grandchild get into a good kindergarten in the fall? Throughout my life the answers more often than not have been to my liking, and I've been able to shoo him out, when that dog of fear and worry has sneaked into my house.

As my father was fond of saying, "I've had trouble all my life, but most of it never happened."

Birthdays

All my life, on the seventh of January, I've become a year older. That used to suit me just fine. Each additional candle on my cake was like a key that could open a new door. This year though, when I woke up on that day I used to love, it came to me that somewhere along the line, birthdays had lost their charm. Turning eighty-seven just didn't have the appeal of, say, turning four when I stayed with my Grandma and Grandpa Palmer, slept in the guest room under a pink satin spread, with flannel sheets and a hot water bottle. Katze, the cat, lay purring beside me, so I wouldn't be lonely. When I reached nine, I got a piano from my parents and the gift of lessons from our neighbor, Mrs. Burdette. The next year my presents included ten books, one of them *Little Women* which I tried to read while drying the dishes.

Remembering all this brought a wave of sadness that almost washed me out to sea. It seemed as though more than anything else, the passage of time meant loss—loss of youth, career, my own home, members of my family, even my ability to walk without a contraption to lean on. I hunkered down in my bed, close to tears. The telephone rang, I reached out to answer it.

"Happy birthday," my five-year-old great-grand-daughter said over the line. "Would you like to go out to the bagel shop with us?" Her little brother was next.

"You can play with my truck," he told me.

After he'd hung up, I got out of bed and took a shower. As the warm water cascaded over my body,

"What's wrong with you anyway?" my mind asked the rest of me. "Remember what Shakespeare said about each person playing many parts in his time? Why don't you think of two things you enjoy in old age that weren't even available when you were young?" The first thing that came up was those great-grandchildren, but I couldn't seem to think of anything else. I climbed out of the shower, sat on the edge of the tub, dried my smooth legs with a big towel. Then it came to me. No longer growing leg hair and having to shave it off every week was certainly not to be undervalued. Maybe getting old wasn't so bad after all!

The Wages of Goodness

January
This year I've decided to be a better person, more
disciplined, less selfish, more intent on caring for this
earth and all the forms of life that call it home. This year
I plan to boycott all those big box stores with their unfair
labor practices, indifference and greed. Nor more
shopping sprees at Wal-mart's, no more overflowing carts
from Toys-R-Us. I'll buy my books from independents,
shun Border like I would a whorehouse. I'll talk, cut back
on gas, eat organic produce, prance past Starbucks with
my nose in the air. I'll get my decafe elsewhere, my
conscience clear as newly polished windows.

December
All year, as I planned, I was a better person, but where
did my virtue get me? It took so much research to sort
the good guys from the bad, that I read no other books
the entire year. I walked till I got a bunion that required
an operation. I hadn't bought good walking shoes,
because I couldn't find a pair not made by ten-year-olds
in China. The fox terrier I got from the pound bit me on
the ankle. My zeal to save the planet inspired some
friends to cross the street when they saw me coming.
Others look right through me since I balked on hanging
the red, white, and blue on Independence Day. Believe
me, folks, being good is not for sissies.

To Sin or Not to Sin

When I was a kid, I was a moderate sinner. At first I couldn't tell what was a sin and what wasn't, but my mom and dad kept me informed. They said killing was the worst one of all, so I carefully avoided that. I wouldn't even swat a fly but did succumb to some of the lower ranking sins on a regular basis. I stole Snickers bars from Woolworths and denied leaving my father's best hammer out in the rain after using it to crack walnuts filched from the neighbors' tree. I also passed the answers to arithmetic test problems to Sam Harris, because I thought he was handsome.

When I was about ten, Harriet Simpson and her family moved two doors down the road from us. For a while, it seemed as though we were going to become best friends. Then one day I asked her if she and her family sinned much.

"What's sin?" she asked.

"It's all that stuff God hates," I told her, "like killing and stealing, drinking beer, smoking, dancing and, of course, playing cards,"

"We don't kill or steal," she said, "but my parents do those other things, except my mother doesn't smoke anymore."

"Does she wear shorts?" I wanted to know.

"Of course, in the summer," she answered. "What's wrong with that?"

"When women show their bare legs, it tempts men to do bad things," I said.

"Such as?" she asked.

"Kiss them," I told her.

"You're kind of weird," she informed me. After that day she just ignored me, like she didn't even know me. And not much later the Simpsons moved back to Los Angeles. Sometimes I wished I could tell Harriet I sold some of my books and with the money bought myself a pair of short shorts that I snuck to school and wore to the end of the class picnic. Then she might have liked me again. She didn't need to know that Sam Harris said I had cute legs.

The Things That You're Liable To Read in the Bible

Some think Eve is to blame for the whole thing, though all she did was offer a forbidden apple to her husband. Adam's the one who scarfed it down like a starving pig. Nowhere does it say she shoved it in his throat against his will. The Bible does say that this world's first couple got their hands' slapped hard for messing around with those apples. Unfair as it seems to me, God decided to punish all future human as well. Eve and all mothers to follow were chastised by pain enough in childbirth to make their shrieking heard a block away. Then they were made second class citizens, subject to the authority of men. Even worse, nobody has been able to evade God's real zinger, inevitable death for all.

Though I'm not crazy about that arrangement, I can see it might be better than having this little planet more over-populated than it is today. But I digress. I do feel kind of sorry for those first human beings. They were just babes in the Garden of Eden with no precedents to follow, not even a good therapist to turn to when things got rough. I feel especially sorry for poor, overworked Eve, with all those kids she and Adam produced during the nearly thousand years of their marriage. When she was 130 years old, she had to have another male child to replace an adult son killed in a fit of jealousy by his brother.

Adam lived 800 years longer, and they had even more offspring. I can just imagine what a picnic that woman's life must have been, taking care of them without the help of Pampers, Gerbers baby food, or even a washing machine. After Adam died when they were 930, she realized that she was tired and her feet hurt. Maybe she should go into a rest home, she decided. But how could she? Who would take care of the baby?

Report Card

This February my obsolete computer got a B
for faithful performance during advanced
old age, the word processor for taking only
nine days of sick leave.

This February the taxi folks flunked out,
with well deserved F-minuses. One driver,
his greasy hat on backwards, drove four miles
in the wrong direction before turning around,
making me late for my doctor's appointment.
The rapidly rising fare flashed in red
on the dashboard, as I insisted my doctor
was not located on the boardwalk. Another cabby
dumped me at the Del Mar Theater for
Mrs. Henderson Presents so late the remaining plot
was clear as a steamy mirror.

This February, there being no higher grade,
I had to give the maker of the best valentine
a mere A-plus. It went, not to Hallmark, but
my four year old great granddaughter. She made
me a crooked paper heart stacked so high
with gold glitter that it left a sparkly path
all the way to my door.

This February I couldn't rank the weather better
than a C. Some days showed promise but lacked
stick-to-it-ness. Trusting folks found themselves
with shoes soggy as a bathmat, wet hair dripping
down their shoulders. The weather needs to be

a better team player, more considerate of those yearning for a picnic.

This February life sometimes gave me the giggles, sometimes clobbered me over the head, sometimes brought me to the knees in gratitude, just as it's apt to do in March, or September, or any other month of the year.

I Didn't Vote For What's His Name

In December I had a stroke,
one that could have been worse,
but was bad enough to cramp
my independent style. My right foot
became weak, requiring the use
of a walker; my right eye went off
in its own direction, making reading difficult;
my memory was as unreliable as the weather
in March. Sometimes I didn't know my age
or the names of all my grandkids.

At the rehabilitation center a speech therapist
tried to help, asking me questions
to encourage recall, which currently
was playing hide and seek. I'd easily
tell my address, only to be unable
to come up with the date. Then
he asked me who the current President was.
That question nearly caused me
to have another stroke. I could feel
my blood pressure rising dangerously.
"The worst President we've ever had,"
I said, "but I can't remember
the guy's name, something like Tree, I think."

"Good job," the therapist said with a big smile.
"I couldn't agree with you more. His name is Bush,
but you got the rest right on the button."

Blame it on Dorothy

My mother was strong on manners. I remember her words, "Always be polite to others, and that includes how you talk on the telephone." In 1925, when I was five, we purchased our first phone, which was fastened over my head on the living room wall. I had to climb up on a chair, dial the operator, and ask her to "Connect me to my Grandma Palmer at 247-J, please." I used equally good manners with my aunts and grandparents as with the operator. Those were the years I listened to what my parents told me and believed every word. "Bring up a child in the way he should go, and when he is old, he will not depart from it", was a Bible verse thoroughly espoused by my parents. As time went by, I departed from the ways they thought God had in mind for me, though when it came to telephone manners, I was a stickler. Until lately anyway. Until Dorothy started ringing me up at dinnertime to offer me a mortgage on the home I do not own, do not ever want to own, either now or in any life to follow. I heard her out night after night with great courtesy. Until last Thursday. That night the devil must have had me in his power, because the moment I heard her cheery voice, just as I'd started to eat, I slammed the phone down, slammed it hard. I've done the same thing every night since. Ahhh—what a freeing experience, what a release, what joy!

About Many Names Press

Many Names Press, founded by printer/poet Kate Hitt in Santa Cruz County, California as an environmentally aware offset and letterpress printing office in 1993, continues to address social, economic and environmental issues through graphic design and award-winning books of lasting quality. Among her many esteemed poets, writers and artists published are: Patrice Vecchione, Amber Coverdale Sumrall, Margarite Tuchardt, Susan Samuels Drake, Andrea Rich, Bill Stipe, Douglas McClellan, Clair Killen, Maude Meehan and Leba Wine. Hermie Medley makes the sixth octogenarian author in this talented group of visionaries.

A list of books for sale are at the website,
www.manynamespress.com/books

Many Names Press/Kate Hitt
P.O. Box 1038 Capitola, CA 95010-1038 USA
khitt@manynamespress.com
831-728-4302